# Time
## to
# Forgive

*...My divine encounter with the angel of Forgiveness*

By

## APOSTLE LEE ROBERSON

*~ Includes: Prayers of Activation ~*

Published by

Author Info:
Apostle Lee Roberson
Sons of God Embassy
Kingsland, Georgia
http://www.sonsofgodministries.net

For Worldwide Distribution Printed in the U.S.A.

# ACKNOWLEDGEMENT

Special thanks to my spiritual parents, Apostle Francis and Carmela Myles, who has been the absolute best leaders and spiritual father and mother to me and my wife. They have been an amazing blessing to my assignment in the body of Christ. They have challenged and encouraged me beyond spoken words. I am forever grateful that my wife and I are connected to these incredible leaders that push all their spiritual children into greatness! Thanks for always being there for me and for inspiring the best out of me. I love you both!

Special thanks to my incredible wife, April Roberson, who is the epitome of Love in every sense of the word. She has been my encourager, motivator, cheerleader and my listener. I am beyond blessed to have such a woman to experience earth and to impact the body of Christ with. Thanks Love for increasing my life. I love you.

# TABLE OF CONTENTS

**CHAPTER ONE:** TIME TO FORGIVE ............... 4

An Encounter with God in India ............... 5

Love or Unforgiveness in Your Cells ............... 7

Get Rid of the Bacteria in Your Soul! ............... 10

Releasing Others ............... 13

The Law of Love ............... 18

**CHAPTER TWO:** PRAYERS OF ACTIVATION ............... 20

The Prayer of Release ............... 20

The Prayer of Forgiving Yourself ............... 21

Prayer to Partner with the
Anti-Bacteria Unforgiveness Angel ............... 21

Prayer of Release of Sickness in Your Body ............... 22

Prayer for Pastors ............... 23

**CHAPTER THREE:** TESTIMONIALS ............... 24

Forgiving your spouse ............... 24

Testimonials ............... 25

# 1

# TIME TO FORGIVE

*"These scriptures are the very foundation of what happened to me in India."*

**Apostle Lee Roberson**

*"For if you forgive men their trespasses, your heavenly Father will also forgive you. But if you do not forgive men their trespasses, neither will your Father forgive your trespasses. Matthew 6:14-15 (NKJV)*

*Therefore if you bring your gift to the altar, and there remember that your brother has something against you, leave your gift there before the altar, and go your way. First be reconciled to your brother, and then come and offer your gift. Matthew 5:23-24 (NKJV)*

# An Encounter with God in India

When God began to minister to me, I was in India. It was October 26, 2017, my second day in India, at approximately 2:00 am. I had this incredible visitation from a very powerful angel and God began to teach me various things about unforgiveness. Now, I know many of us have heard about unforgiveness, we've taught about it many times, I've taught on it many times but I've never encountered such a powerful experience before that changed my life in this way. Before I get into the vision, there are a few quick points that I want to bring to your attention. The first thing you need to understand is that when mankind was born, his original birthplace was love. So, when we were born, we were born from love and into love. Whenever you walk in unforgiveness, you move yourself from your original birthplace. Secondly, whenever we walk in unforgiveness, the love that we perceive that we are giving to people is tainted; that love is not pure because you have an aught against another brother or a sibling. In fact, Jesus put it this way in Luke 6:32: *"But if you love those who love you, what credit is that to you? For even sinners love those who love them" (NKJV)*. So it's easy to love people who love you. But what about those that have hurt you or offended you? The ones that have done you wrong?

I was in India when I had this experience. It was the second day going into the third. It was the morning of the third day and my room was filled with the presence of the Lord. It was 2 o'clock in the morning and I was taken into an open vision. I began to see myself walking down this road and as I was walking down this road, I took note of the surroundings. It seemed like an evening day; it was not quite dark but approaching night. It was a clear day with evening air. After walking for a short time, I noticed to my left there was a building. It was a small building, a very nice-shaped building but I immediately knew in the open vision as I was walking that this building was a bathroom. I walked off the road towards the building and as I began to walk into the door, I noticed a man standing to my left who was of great size and great stature. I didn't have any thought about it, I just noticed him and then I went into the bathroom. When I went into the bathroom, I immediately noticed that there was a man in a wheelchair and I couldn't help but think to myself, *"How is this man going to get out of the wheelchair and use the restroom."* As soon as I thought that, the man that was outside came into the bathroom. I knew at that point that was not a man but it was an angel. Keep in mind; this is a one stall bathroom and it was just me and the man in the wheelchair. When the angel came inside the bathroom, he turned to me and smiled. When he smiled, me and the man in the wheelchair were outside of the bathroom but the man was no longer in the wheelchair; he was standing on his feet. If you've ever been in an open vision, you know that you don't talk through your mouth, it's just thought. So I knew immediately who this angel was or at least I *thought* I knew who he was. The man that was in the wheelchair turned to me as if to ask me who he was so I turned to the man and said to him, "Oh, that's the Angel of Unforgiveness!" The angel turned to me and said to me, "No! My name is Anti-Bacteria Unforgiveness Angel!" And when he said that, the thought began to develop in my mind *"I've never heard of you before"* so I immediately began to challenge what he said. As soon as I began to challenge him, he challenged me back with Hebrews 12:22 which says, *"But you have come to Mount Zion and to the city of the living God, the heavenly Jerusalem, to an innumerable company of angels"* and I immediately knew that we have angels that we have never even met before. When I said that, the angel turned to me with this huge, massive white gun but it was not a gun like you and I are familiar with. This gun did not fire bullets; this was an instrument I had never seen before on planet Earth. This was something that only heaven could manifest! With a look of joy upon his face, he turned to me with this massive gun and immediately started shooting inside of my body cells...yes, cells! They were incredible cells! Cells of all colors! I'm sure that most of you have seen pictures of cells that are inside of our bodies. As these cells left this massive machine, I took note that they were perfect in shape and alive and the colors that were on each one was alive. Yes, you heard me correctly; the cells were full of life and the colors that were on them were full of life. I watched each cell and its color; there were colors I had never seen before and when they hit my body, my body began to respond immediately. My body began to be refreshed, there was energy coming into my body, my body began to swell with a strength that had been absent for a while and I got this feeling that they were replacing cells that had been destroyed. And immediately, I had strength in my body! Folks, I can tell you, the cells that you see on pictures are not even close to the original cells that go into your body... they're not even close! The colors, the perfect shape and each cell has the life of God inside of it.

## Love or Unforgiveness in Your Cells

I immediately came out of the vision and I begin to look up pictures of cells and I called my wife. Now, this is about

3 o'clock in the morning. I called my wife, who was in America, and I began to tell her about the experience that I had. Now I want you to hold onto this because this is very powerful: God began to teach me some powerful things about the Body of Christ. When I called my wife, she began to rejoice and she said to me, "I have to share something with you." I said, "What is it?" She said, "I just had a dream." Now keep in mind, I'm in India, she's in America. She said that in the dream, she was laying in the bed and she turned to where I usually sleep and there was a man in the bed and he was dead! Are you hearing what I'm saying? She said the man in the bed was dead! She said in the dream, she screamed out and she called to me and said, "Chris, come get this dead man out of the bed!" She said that she got up and went around and touched the dead man's feet. And when she told me all of this, she asked me, "What does this mean"? I told her that I didn't know then I said, "Let me call you right back" because I could still feel the presence of God and the room was still charged. As soon I hung up with my wife, I went right back into the vision and the angel began to teach me more stuff about the cells, about unforgiveness. He said, "Study my name!" Now remember what the angel said his name was….he said his name was Anti-Bacteria Unforgiveness Angel. As I began to study the angel's name, my wife's dream was occupying my mind so I did a search and found a piece that stated when you forgive, you move from "SPIRITUAL DEATH" to "FRUITFULNESS." I knew the answer and I said to myself, "The man that was in the bed was me!" I emailed my wife the information that I had found and my wife replied to my email saying, "Yea, I didn't want to tell you but the man that was in the bed was the same size as you." After the revelation given by the Anti-Bacteria Unforgiveness Angel,

I knew that I had not forgiven my wife. So I called her back immediately but there was something different now; I could feel it deep down in my inner man. There was a new energy and strength, a cleanliness that was not there prior to the angel releasing those cells into my body. I said to my wife, "I forgive you" and we both rejoiced! I noticed how much easier it was to forgive now that I had been impacted by the angel. I also noticed how pure and clean and so full of love the forgiveness was. See, after the angel fired those new cells into my body, it became easier to forgive and it felt so very natural to do so.

After I finished speaking to my wife, God began to speak to me and said these words: "There are a lot of dead men in My body; there are a lot of dead women in My body because they're walking in unforgiveness. They do not understand, the Church does not understand the power of unforgiveness." See, prior to me going to India to minister, my wife and I got into this heated and very ugly fight that caused both of us to say very, very harsh words to one another. These words penetrated my heart and I never forgave my wife. So, in the sight of God, I was a dead man because I failed to forgive.

Folks, when you walk in unforgiveness, you are spiritually dead to God! I began to do research and the angel began to walk me through his name: his name was Anti-Bacteria Unforgiveness Angel. *Anti* means "to be against" or "opposed." Now, when he said bacteria, he called it "unforgiveness bacteria." I did more research and I found out that a bacteria is a living organism. I also found out that one of the first things that they discovered in man's body was bacteria. Now, this is going to blow your mind: a bacteria kills cells two (2) different ways. Now, every time

I say bacteria, I want you to equate it to unforgiveness because that's what he called unforgiveness...bacteria. Scientists and doctors have proven that unforgiveness is responsible for high blood pressure, diabetes, cancer, depression...even arthritis! The angel began to walk me through this and he showed me where unforgiveness has been destroying cells in our bodies that were put in our bodies *to help us to forgive*! Are you hearing what I'm saying? The number one question that I ask most people when I teach on forgiveness is "how many have trouble forgiving? How many want to forgive but don't know how to forgive?" And many hands go in the air. It is because these unforgiveness bacteria have killed the cells that help you to forgive! God spoke to me and said, "It is unnatural for you to walk in unforgiveness."

## GET RID OF THE BACTERIA IN YOUR SOUL!

I began to do more research on bacteria; remember bacteria kills cells two (2) different ways. The main way that bacteria kills cells is that it infiltrates the cells, it goes inside the cell, and it eats the cell until it dies. That's the number one way that bacteria kills cells. The second way that bacteria kills cells is that it releases toxins and poisons that kill cells. So think on this. What does unforgiveness carry that is toxic and poisonous? (1) Bitterness (2) Resentment (3) Revenge and (4) Rage. Another thing that is fascinating about a bacteria is that it has a membrane and an outer wall or shell. That means that bacteria can lay dormant inside of you. Remember, when I say bacteria, think unforgiveness. Here's the most powerful thing about the outside wall of the bacteria: it protects the bacteria against extreme conditions. That's powerful! That means that unforgiveness protects itself against extreme conditions. So what would be extreme conditions against unforgiveness? You're walking in unforgiveness and somebody shows up and tries to love you, tries to show you kindness, tries to help you and be there for you…that's extreme conditions to unforgiveness! The bacteria quickly goes into a protective mode to keep you bitter, hostile and short with people who are there to simply love you. So the outer shell of the bacteria (unforgiveness) fights against the love and kindness and keeps it from entering into your body so you won't be able to forgive. The second thing about the bacteria is the most powerful thing of all….it can feed itself. So after it has destroyed a cell, bacteria can actually lie dormant and feed itself. The angel was teaching me that unforgiveness feeds itself and it keeps itself alive inside of us so we don't forgive. So how does it feed itself? It keeps bitterness coming inside of us; grudge is feeding it; protecting yourself, not mingling, not allowing touching, not allowing conversation to deal with what happened. That's what it's doing; unforgiveness is lying dormant in you and protecting itself and keeping you in unforgiveness. It knows that if it can keep you in unforgiveness, it moves you from your original birthplace, which is love.

I began to go deeper and the angel began to show me how the Body of Christ is moving and he said to me, "Son, don't look at people's gifts and judge them by their gifts thinking that they are in right standing with me. You can still use your gifts; your gifts are given to you without repentance so you can still flow in your gifts and *still* be walking in unforgiveness." Jesus said in Matthew 7:22-23, *"Many will say to Me in that day, 'Lord, Lord, have we not prophesied in Your name, cast out demons in Your name, and done many wonders in Your name?' And then I will*

*declare to them, 'I never knew you; depart from Me...'"*
And God began to minister to me and said, "There are a lot of dead bodies in My body." A few days later, He spoke these words to me, "Son, it's time for the Body of Christ to forgive! You tell everybody that you teach this to, tell them, the first thing that they have to do is release the people that did them wrong in relationships. People have been holding grudges." He said, "Make sure you specifically tell pastors around the world that they work hard but people take advantage of them, people lie to them, they take them for granted, they use your anointing and then they leave! And it's not that you wish anything bad on them but you hold a grudge for how they left." And I began to release people that left my house, who did me wrong. I began to release them and it began to bring freedom to me. God specifically told me to tell my house (and you) to sit down over the next 2 months and this angel is going to help you and minister to you. He's going to begin to show you people that you need to release. There are people that we've been carrying that we've never released. There are people that are stuck in us that we've never let go. There is trauma that we've been carrying for years but we didn't know how to forgive. But now there's an angel that's been released from heaven called the Anti-Bacteria Unforgiveness Angel and he's ready to replace the cells that have been destroyed by this bacteria called unforgiveness! I'm telling you saints of God, I began to go closer and deeper in this. He said, "Come! Let me show you something!" He showed me the bacteria! He said, "Watch this! When Adam and Eve fell, Adam blamed God." Adam blamed God for Eve; he said, "....that woman you gave me." And then Eve said, "The serpent...." But you never saw or read in the Scripture where Adam or Eve asked for forgiveness. Remember the

lame man that they brought to Jesus and He said to him, "Thy sins are forgiven you?" (Mark 2) Remember that? He said to the man, "Thy sins are forgiven you and the man was healed and got up!" And at first they were mad because they said who can forgive sin? And the Lord began to walk me through the scriptures and He said, "Each time I said that, the person that was sick was sick because they were walking in unforgiveness. Remember the man in the restroom with me that was in the wheelchair? That man was in the wheelchair because of unforgiveness. Sickness is in people's body because of unforgiveness. If you forgive, the sickness will leave your body, in Jesus' mighty name!

Now this is going to bless you! I want you to hear me! When God commissioned them in the spirit, He said, "Bless **them**! Be fruitful and multiply!" He said, "Bless **them** and be fruitful and multiply! He was talking about Adam and Eve. And then He blew my mind! He said, "What was the last thing that Jesus said? Jesus said these words, "Father, forgive **them** for they know not what they've done." God told me, "You teach that Jesus was saying forgive them that killed Him and that's true. But He was really saying forgive Adam and Eve for what they did. See, His forgiveness had to reach back to where man first sinned. This guaranteed that our past couldn't run us down and demand payment. They introduced us to an era and to a time of walking in unforgiveness. Unforgiveness is the only spirit that can keep us from walking in agape love. Unforgiveness is the single thing responsible for the blessing slipping through the hands of the people about to receive it.

## RELEASING OTHERS

Then, God began to show me something powerful...

watch this! He said, "The first thing I would do is I would challenge you to see if you understand that I really forgave you." I said, "What do you mean?" He said, "Go to Matthew 18:27-28." *Then the master of that servant was moved with compassion, released him, and forgave him the debt. "But that servant went out and found one of his fellow servants who owed him a hundred denarii; and he laid hands on him and took him by the throat, saying, 'Pay me what you owe!'* God said, "The first thing that I do is once I forgive you, I now ask you to release somebody who owes you!" The reason He told me He does that is to see if you *really* understand the *value* of forgiveness. "I will challenge your level of forgiveness. I will always bring someone back to you who did you wrong and I'm going to see how you treat them. I've forgiven you; now it's time for you to forgive them!" He does that to see if the bacteria was destroyed in you…unforgiveness. Now you have an opportunity to forgive but you don't forgive, therefore, unforgiveness goes back into a dormant state inside of us.

Now, here's the most powerful thing about a bacteria; it has a membrane and an outer wall. Why is that important? The membrane does 3 powerful things: 1. it separates the bacteria from the other cells; 2. it controls what goes in and out of the bacteria and 3. it protects the bacteria. Are you hearing what God is saying? He's saying the membrane of the bacteria separates itself from the other cells because the other cells help you to forgive! So unforgiveness keeps itself away from the other cells that will help you to forgive people. Then, it goes into protective mode and keeps it from receiving true love, true kindness so that bitterness and harshness and grudges remain inside of you. God said to me that most people that are walking in unforgiveness will act as if they've forgiven and they will make statements like this: "Oh, I forgave them!" But God said to me, "True forgiveness means that you have granted the person that hurt you access back into your life." I'm going to say that again: *true* forgiveness means that the person that hurt you has free access back into your life. I didn't say that they could do the same thing to you but they should be able to have free access back into your life because God said, "If I forgave you, did you not have free access back into Me?" So if you find yourself protecting yourself against that person, you have not forgiven. Then He said, "Unforgiveness infects the love that you release to everyone else." You think you are loving people but you are loving them to keep you from the other party that hurt you. See, that's your way of staying away from or not dealing with it. Now here's the danger of that: that gives unforgiveness permission to lay dormant in you and the longer it lays dormant in you, the deader you are. I was *dead*! I was *dead*! The *apostle* was dead! And before the angel came and shot cells back into my body, I was preaching, teaching, flowing in the gifts but dead! You can't go off of your teaching, you can't go off of your gifts and you can't go off of your talents because they are given to you without repentance. But if you do not forgive, your Father will not forgive you and you are spiritually dead! This is why you can't get enough. This is why when you try to collect, you don't collect enough. This is why you try to flow but you don't flow enough because there's some unforgiveness, there are some grudges. Believe me, I know because I come from a family that holds grudges. But I'm telling you, by the Spirit of the living God, if you will receive when I pray, this angel is going to begin to minister to you and he's going to begin to restore cells back into your body that have been destroyed by this bacteria called unforgiveness. If you will receive today, you'll release that man that hurt you years ago; you'll release that one that molested you many years ago; you'll release the one that left you; you'll release the one that abandoned you; you'll begin to release them and the angel will begin to restore cells back into your body!

You need to understand…God created us as a cellular structure. Our whole body is a big cellular structure! So that means that when God designed us, He designed us to walk in incredible love. Now, that means that there were cells that gave us energy and help to forgive. But what unforgiveness does is it destroys those cells - they eat 'em! So that's why you don't have the *energy*. That's why it's easy for you to say, "I'll never forgive them. I don't care what they do. I'll never let them go. I'll never forgive them!" Why? Because the cells that were giving you energy to forgive have been eaten up by unforgiveness. Then God told me this, he said, "Son, I want you to pay attention! How you love is a direct reflection of how you love yourself." I said, "What do you mean?" He said, "The way you love everyone else is a direct reflection of how you love yourself." So then, if you walk in unforgiveness, it's the proof that you really don't love you. You're mad at you for letting yourself get in that predicament! You're really mad at you for allowing yourself to be taken advantage of. If you can't love them, it's the proof that you don't really love yourself. This is why Jesus said, "Love your neighbors as you love yourself." That's powerful! So that means if I've got a "love problem," I've got an "unforgiveness problem." It's not the other person, it's really me.

I want to show you guys the True Love. The Father said to me, "Watch the two final things My Son did before He exited the earth to return to Me. Son, You must understand,

I sent You from Me in love so You must return in the same spirit." He takes me to Jesus' last moments on Earth as a man and He says, "Watch closely!" Jesus is exchanged for one called Barabbas who was being held in prison for (1) robbery and (2) murder/rebellion. Barabbas' name means: Son of Abba. The Father speaks to me and says, "Son, when Jesus was exchanged for Barabbas, it was Me pardoning (forgiving) mankind (Adam/Eve) for (1) robbing me (tithes). The tree they ate from was tithes; it was the only tree that Adam was commanded to stay away from. He could eat from every other tree but not that one because that tree was tithes. God was also forgiving mankind for (2) murder/rebellion. Adam murdered all of mankind from walking in Diety and introduced us all to humanity. Let me explain. When Adam was created, he was all divine in his Diety State which means he was all supreme power on earth. He had a body but none of the weaknesses we see today or feel today. Adam only experienced supreme power with no participation from his flesh (humanity). He was just like his creator but with a glorified body. So, when God told him in Gen 2:17, "the day you eat from that tree you shall surely die" and he ate from the tree, he robbed us all from experiencing that supreme state called Diety; instead, we now experience humanity first then we are born into our divine nature. So when Jesus was exchanged for Barabbas, it was Me announcing to mankind, "I forgive you and give you total access back into your Kingdom!" The most important words came from the mouth that God wrapped in His Son's body: "Father, forgive them for they know not what they do." So as you can see, forgiveness allows us to return to our first state and original birth place which is love. Each time you forgive, it's an act of love and the revealing of the Father's heart. This is why the adversary desires for us to remain in unforgiveness; he knows that it robs us of this powerful revelation of walking in agape love. This brings us to the most important Law of them all: The Law of Love. See folks, unforgiveness was so strong on planet Earth that in many ways it had become like a Law meaning many of us felt we had a *right* not to forgive people, that we had a *right* to hold bitterness in our hearts. Based upon how we were treated by the other party and depending on the advice we received from people who were not walking in Godly council or Godly love (agape love), we let unforgiveness remain dormant in our heart. So, to replace or destroy a Law, a greater one must be created. So this is where Jesus our Lord comes in. He is not going to become love, He is love and so when Mary conceived Jesus, she conceived love. When she birthed Jesus in the Earth, the Law of Love was born and is now active in the Earth.

## THE LAW OF LOVE

"The Law of Love is this: if Jesus had never died, then the Law of Love could not be established in the Earth. This is why Jesus, before His departure, gathered His disciples for a very important message that He delivered in John 13:34-35: I give you a *new* Law and that Law is to love each other. As I have loved you, so you also love each other. This is how all people will know that you are my disciples. Wow, I don't know about you but these words just jump off the page now that I have met this incredible angel, the Anti-Bacteria Unforgiveness Angel. Jesus' words to His disciples and to us now is that we are recognized by the depth of our love for each other. And the one thing that stops the love that Jesus gave us back is this spirit called unforgiveness. But we have one greater. Let us abide in this incredible Law of Love so that when we are wronged, hurt badly, betrayed, abused and mistreated, we will still be full of agape love and this will allow us to forgive on demand! Can you imagine being able to forgive on demand?! I don't know about you but I think this would be an incredible achievement! It is a reachable goal because of our Lord Jesus' obedience to death. Now we have no excuse! We have His Spirit, we have His Words and we have His nature and now they are at work in you. IT'S TIME TO FORGIVE!

So now, as you and I come into agreement with the prayers that you are about to pray, receive that agape love and allow the Holy Spirit to minister to you, along with the Anti-Bacteria Unforgiveness Angel. Allow them to bring you to complete healing and restoration from this bacteria called forgiveness. May the Spirit of Christ be upon you in an incredible way as you go forward in Jesus' name. Amen!!

# 2

# PRAYERS OF ACTIVATION

*Put Me in remembrance; Let us contend together; State your case, that you may be acquitted. Isaiah 43:26*

## THE PRAYER OF RELEASE

Heavenly Father, I come before Your Holy Courtroom today. I am seeking forgiveness from You. First, let me repent for walking in unforgiveness. I lift Your Word before You according to Matthew 6:14-15 that states if I forgive men of their trespasses, You will forgive me but if I forgive not men of their trespasses, neither will You forgive me of my trespasses. Today Lord, I am ready to forgive and release from my heart the individual or individuals that has been occupying it. In the name of Jesus Christ, Father I forgive (call out the name of the person/people who you need to forgive) and I release them. Father, I forgive them in the name of Jesus Christ. I forgive the pain and the hurt that has been caused by this individual. I forgive them and I restore them in the name of Jesus Christ. And Father, I thank You now that Your Spirit is coming upon me to help me to release them and completely forgive them. Now Father, as I have forgiven them, I receive Your forgiving power that will release me from the spirit of unforgiveness that I've been walking in. I receive it now. In Jesus' name, Amen!

## THE PRAYER OF FORGIVING YOURSELF

Heavenly Father, I thank You that I now fully understand that I am worthy of forgiveness. So therefore, I forgive myself for holding myself hostage, for causing myself pain and affliction because I have not forgiven myself. Today, I gladly receive Your forgiveness and I gladly receive the blessing of Jesus Christ, the blood that causes me to be worthy. So I release myself and I release myself from the spirit of condemnation and the spirit of feeling unworthy. I accept my value through Jesus Christ my Lord. I forgive myself! In Jesus' name, Amen.

## PRAYER TO PARTNER WITH THE ANTI-BACTERIA UNFORGIVENESS ANGEL

Heavenly Father, I thank You that according to Hebrews 1:14 Your Word says, "are they not all ministering spirits sent forth to minister to them who are the heirs of salvation?" Lord, thank You that through Jesus Christ, I am the heir of salvation and I thank You that You have released in the earth realm and the Body of Christ this incredible angel named Anti-Bacteria Unforgiveness Angel. I position myself right now because I have forgiven and because I have released and because I have restored the individual(s) and because I have granted them access back into my life.

Now I partner with the Anti-Bacteria Unforgiveness Angel that he may now restore to me all the cells that have been destroyed, that have been full of toxins, that have been full of poison and those that have been damaged badly because of unforgiveness. I give him permission to release unto me right now the cells that I originally had that will cause me to not only walk in Your agape love but to not hold any offenses, any grudges, any bitterness. I receive now in Jesus' name Your ministering angel, the Anti-Bacteria Unforgiveness Angel. I receive the new cells that have replaced those that have been destroyed by unforgiveness. In Jesus' name, Amen!

## PRAYER OF RELEASE OF SICKNESS IN YOUR BODY

Father, right now, because the person listening to this has fully submitted to Your Word and partnered with Your angel, Anti-Bacteria Unforgiveness Angel, the spirit of unforgiveness has been destroyed in their life and in their heart. I take authority now and I command all sickness that has previously occupied their body because of unforgiveness to be destroyed. I command high blood pressure, sickle cell, diabetes, arthritis, blood clots, all sickness and disease that had legal right to occupy the body because of unforgiveness, you are now destroyed! I command you to release this body and not return. I command Isaiah 53:5 and I Peter 2:24 to have free reign to run through this body, touch every organ, touch every cell, touch every tissue now and bring complete healing through Jesus Christ our Lord. We give Your name glory and honor and we thank You today that unforgiveness has no root in our heart. In Jesus' name, Amen!

# PRAYER FOR PASTORS

Pastors, God spoke to me and said to lead you through this prayer because of how many have treated you and left you. We have, in many cases, developed grudges and hard hearts. So Pastors, this prayer is for you:

Heavenly Father, I come before You and I desire to release all grudges and disappointments I have with individuals in my heart. I release all grudges I have in my heart for individuals that have left my ministry the wrong way. I also forgive all accusations and false words spoken against me and the ministry that You have given me. Father, I forgive all the individuals that made promises but didn't keep them and release them through the spirit of forgiveness and the expectation of the fulfillment of the promise. I gladly release and forgive all individuals who have taken members away from this ministry and forgive them and release them from my heart. Now Father, I position myself for Your forgiveness to fall in my ministry so that those that are here may experience Your agape love and that this ministry may operate in the fullness of Your Spirit. Now I bless those that have chosen to pursue You in other places and houses. May Your Spirit lead them and protect them and bring them to Your expected end for them. In Jesus' name, Amen!

# 3

# TESTIMONIALS

*And they overcame him by the blood of the Lamb and by the word of their testimony, and they did not love their lives to the death. Revelation 12:11*

## FORGIVING YOUR SPOUSE

After the revelation given by the Anti-Bacteria Unforgiveness Angel, I knew that I had not forgiven my wife. So I called her back immediately but there was something different now; I could feel it deep down in my inner man. There was a new energy and strength, a cleanliness that was not there prior to the angel releasing those cells into my body. I said to my wife, "I forgive you" and we both rejoiced! I noticed how much easier it was to forgive now that I had been impacted by the angel. I also noticed how pure and clean and so full of love the forgiveness was. See, after the angel fired those new cells into my body, it became easier to forgive and it felt so very natural to do so. The testimonials below will help you appreciate the "Value of forgiveness."

## TESTIMONIALS

After Apostle Robinson got back from India, he shared with us what the Anti-Bacteria Unforgiveness had given him during our Morning Prayer line. He told us what had happened in his vision. Before this revelation, I never thought I had issues with unforgiveness but God showed me what was really in my heart. I began to examine myself and saw what was really inside. It was then that I cried out to God and He restored my heart.

Shortly after, I went to visit my older siblings; I saw my two sisters on Thanksgiving Day and my brothers a few days later. I told them that I forgave them and asked them to forgive me, as well. I grabbed their hands and we prayed. With great excitement, I began to share with others what God had done for me. One morning, while sitting at the information desk, this woman walked past me. I spoke to her and asked how she was doing. She spoke back and continued on out the door. A few minutes later, she came back and called my name and I acknowledged that it was me. She said, "You don't remember me, do you?" I have to admit at first I didn't. She told me who she was and I got up, walked over to her, wrapped my arms around her and asked how she had been. I told that I was glad to see her and asked how everyone was doing. I must have really startled her. The last time I laid eyes on her was at my father's funeral and before. Right before my father died, she had had me banned from the hospital.

I am so thankful for what God gave Apostle Lee Roberson! My life has not been the same. I now share with others who are asking for this book.

*Sharon Dixon, Alabama*


God is definitely revealing, delivering and moving among His sons! This teaching truly blessed me! That morning before church, God continued to bring people before me; those who hurt, offended, even molested me. I asked why because I thought I was past that phase of my life. When I got to church and received this teaching, I immediately called each person by name and forgave them. Each name I called out, I felt a weight lift off my shoulders. I actually felt free! Since that teaching, God has revealed to me that He has a purpose for everyone. That which was meant to harm us, God will use for our good and to help others overcome the same battles! Hallelujah!!

*Jacqueline Fair, Georgia*


There are so many profound benefits to forgiveness but the one that stood out the most was that if we walk in unforgiveness, we are spiritually dead to God and that the agape love that we think we are giving to people is tainted. The breakdown of how the cells of unforgiveness work as a bacteria versus how new cells of love work after being shot into us by God's love gun also stood out to me. I also appreciated knowing how the root of unforgiveness got into the earthly realm by Adam and Eve not asking for forgiveness for their disobedience in the Garden. These facts are fire from God that fall onto everyone that I let listen to Apostle Lee Roberson's visit with the Anti-Bacteria Unforgiveness

Angel. It saturates the person's spirit so that it becomes more sensitive and has a keen awareness of the warning signals and red flags of unforgiveness.

My nephew and niece's marriage was falling apart. She had moved him out. Both listened separately to the vision. I got a text from my niece. Her husband had written out his decree that he was no longer walking in unforgiveness. He was ready to do what he needed to do to make his marriage work. He is going to rehab! He had been fighting alcoholism without God. He had also started taking Xanax. This is one of my tools that I take on every assignment now!

*Ladina Willis, Arizona*

Made in the USA
Columbia, SC
01 November 2021

47956619R00017